CATSHILL

Public Record Office
Pocket Guides to Family History

Getting Started in Family History

Using Birth, Marriage and Death Records

Using Census Returns

Using Wills

Using Army Records

Using Navy Records

USING CENSUS RETURNS

PUBLIC RECORD OFFICE

Public Record Office
Richmond
Surrey
TW9 4DU

ISBN 1 873162 89 8

A catalogue card for this book
is available from the British Library

Front cover: family group of the Lowes and the Harveys,
Wednesbury, 28 March 1901 (PRO COPY 1/450)

Printed by Cromwell Press Ltd, Trowbridge, Wilts.

CONTENTS

INTRODUCTION

Before you can search the censuses, you need to have got back about 100 years in your family history. You can't consult census records until they are 100 years old. You must also have some idea of where your family were living then.

The censuses can take you back as far as 1841 with firm data, and back further than that by following the evidence given in 1841. They should give you a much deeper knowledge of who your family were and what their lives were like. You can make new discoveries of family members and find out what they did for a living, and whom they lived with. You may also catch a glimpse of the society in which they lived – their wider family, their neighbours, and their neighbourhood.

This Pocket Guide tells you what the census was and how it evolved. It explains

- where you can go to make your search of the census returns

- what information you can expect to find

- the various research tools and how to use them

Census records give valuable information on your
ancestors' occupations and who they lived with.
Group of servants at Squerreys Lodge,
Westerham, Kent, 25 May 1892
(PRO COPY 1/408)

WHAT IS A CENSUS?

A census is a survey of a population taken on a particular date, together with a statistical analysis of the results. In the British Isles the census is based largely on the household as a unit (with provision made for those living in different kinds of communities and institutions).

The census was not intended as a source for family historians, and therefore it has not been organised in the most convenient way for our purposes. Censuses are taken to gather information for use in planning, and in monitoring concerns of interest to the government of the day. The information in it was used at the time of creation to study trends in public health, migration from country to city, alterations in the average age of the populace, changes in work patterns and so on. Historians also study these and other subjects, and the census is one of the major sources for local history.

Census taking and census promises

A national census is taken throughout the UK every ten years. England and Wales (taken here to include the Channel Islands and the Isle of Man) and Scotland have had a census every ten years since 1801 (except in 1941). In Ireland the census started in 1821.

The census was taken on a single designated census night. The head of each household was legally obliged to provide the required information about each person staying in the household on this night. This included everyone present, even those who were visiting.

In order to encourage the people taking part to be truthful, an assurance is given at each census that the detailed returns will be kept secret for 100 years. For this reason the 1891 census returns are the latest that can be searched until 2002, when the 1901 census returns are opened for research.

The organisation of census taking evolved gradually. A general rule applies that the later the date of the census, the fuller and more accurate it is likely to be.

WHICH CENSUSES CAN BE SEARCHED?

Census returns from 1921 onward for the United Kingdom cannot be searched for information on individuals. In the Republic of Ireland, the census of 1926 is already open and can be searched at the National Archives in Dublin.

The 1911 census

The 1911 census for England, Wales and Scotland will not open for inspection until January 2012. The only exception is if you can prove a legal need to consult the 1911 census (on the grounds that there is a legal requirement for information that is not available anywhere else). A search can then be done on your behalf. Application forms are available at the Family Records Centre (FRC) (see pp. 22–5).

The 1911 census for the whole of Ireland is now open, and can be searched at the National Archives in Dublin.

The 1901 census

The 1901 census for England, Wales and Scotland is closed until January 2002. Until then, exceptions are allowed for direct descendants of the person whose census record is to be revealed, or the next of kin if there are no surviving direct descendants. Requests for the age and place of birth of a specifically named person staying at an exact address can be submitted on application forms available from the Family Records Centre.

In January 2002, the 1901 census will be opened in an entirely new way – on the internet. Searching the 1901 census will be much easier than searching earlier censuses. It will be available wherever there is access to the internet, and it will be much easier to find your family members within it. There is likely to be a fee, but the whole business will be transformed into something much quicker and simpler to do. It will be indexed, and the index entries will link directly to images of the relevant pages. You will also be able to read through a census return page by page. Local record offices will be able to buy copies of the 1901 census on microfiche, as they do for earlier censuses.

The 1901 census for the whole of Ireland is now open, and can be searched at the National Archives in Dublin.

The 1891–1841 censuses

These censuses are open to public inspection. Copies of local areas are widely available, and the full set for England and Wales can be seen at the Family Records Centre in London. The full set for Scotland can be seen at the General Register Office for Scotland, in Edinburgh.

Irish censuses before 1901 do not survive, with rare exceptions. The returns for the 1861–91 censuses were destroyed (as being of no interest), by administrators. Those for the 1841 and 1851 censuses were largely destroyed by fire in 1922. For a list of surviving census returns, see Gibson and Medlycott, *Local Census Listings, 1522–1930*. There was no Irish census before 1821.

The undermentioned Houses are situate within the Boundaries of the

*Civil Parish [or Township] of ... Municipal Borough of Sheffield ... Municipal Ward of ... Parliamentary Borough of Sheffield ... Village or Hamlet, &c. of ... Local Board, or [Improvement Commissioners District] of Sheffield ... Ecclesiastical District of St George's

No. of Schedule	ROAD, STREET, &c., and No. or NAME of HOUSE	HOUSES Inhabited / Uninhabited (U.), or Building (B.)	NAME and Surname of each Person	RELATION to Head of Family	CON-DITION	AGE of Males / Females	Rank, Profession, or OCCUPATION	WHERE BORN	Whether 1. Deaf-and-Dumb 2. Blind 3. Imbecile or Idiot 4. Lunatic
113	4.5 Victoria St	1		Head				Yorkshire, Sheffield	Blind Partially
114	4.5"	1							
115	4.7	1							
116	4.9	1							
117	50 Victoria St	1							

Total of Houses .. 4   Total of Males and Females ..

* Draw the pen through such of the words as are inappropriate.

1871 census return for Victoria Street, Sheffield (PRO RG 10/4677, f.75ᵛ)

The 1881 census is currently the easiest one to use, because it has been indexed by name. If you have traced your family back this far using civil registration certificates, or if you have just the name of a family and the county where they lived, you will almost certainly be able to track them here. For more information, read on!

The Scots are even better off, for the 1881 census returns for Scotland have been computerised, and are available on the internet, for a fee: see pp. 26 and 60–61.

The 1831–1801 censuses

The 1801 census was the first national census in England, Wales and Scotland. Unfortunately, these censuses are of little use to family historians. Names weren't collected, and in general all that remains is statistics.

The enumerators (census data collectors) compiled an official return by sex, family and occupation. The total number of houses in each parish was also recorded together with how many were empty. Information on baptisms, marriages and deaths was also gathered. Once the information had been compiled it was gathered centrally, analysed and published in the form of census reports, presented to Parliament in the Parliamentary Papers. The returns used to compile the Parliamentary Papers were destroyed in 1904, as they were thought to be of no further use. Parliamentary Papers can be consulted in the Public

Record Office at Kew (PRO), and elsewhere. Although they do not contain any information about individuals, they can give you a picture of the overall community to which your family belonged.

However, some enumerators did keep a record of names to help them in their task, and a few of these records survive. They are most likely to be found in the local record office of the area where the enumerator was working. It is worth checking in Chapman, *Pre-1841 Censuses and Population Listings* and Gibson and Medlycott, *Local Census Listings, 1522–1930* to see whether you are lucky enough to have ancestors who were mentioned in these records. Local record offices can be found in the telephone directory, or by checking *Record Repositories in Great Britain* or Gibson and Peskett, *Record Offices and How to Find Them*.

There was no Irish census before 1821. The returns for the 1821 and 1831 censuses were largely destroyed by fire in 1922. For a list of surviving census returns, see Gibson and Medlycott, *Local Census Listings, 1522–1930*.

Earlier local censuses

There was a long tradition of census taking in the British Isles before the 19th century. Different kinds of censuses were taken at different times in many small localities for a variety of purposes. Sometimes only heads were counted in a particular parish, and sometimes more detailed information was gathered about a community, perhaps in order to distribute money left to charity. These censuses were organised and carried out locally as required. If any record of them survives, it is likely to be found in the local record office of the area where the count took place. Useful sources for finding early censuses are Chapman, *Pre 1841 Censuses and Population Listings* and Gibson and Medlycott, *Local Census Listings, 1522–1930*.

WHERE TO GO
TO SEARCH THE CENSUS

The original census returns are not available to the general public because of the damage that continual handling would cause. Instead they have been photographed and made available as microfilm or microfiche.

- Microfilm is a long strip of film that has sequential pages of original documents photographed onto it in separate frames. The film is kept in rolls and is read on a machine, which magnifies each frame in turn as you wind the film along.

- Microfiche are strips of microfilm that have been cut and arranged in sequential rows into a form similar to an index card. They avoid the need to wind the film.

Using microfilm or microfiche versions means that you can search the census at more than one site. However, the national archives of each country (i.e. England and Wales; Scotland; Northern Ireland; and Ireland) keep the full sets for that country, so if you want to trace ancestors who lived in different parts of Britain and Ireland from you, this is the place to go. The national sets also usually have a fuller range of indexes and other finding aids. You can search the census records at:

- Local record offices and county libraries (incomplete sets)

- Family History Centres (films need to be ordered)

- The Family Records Centre, London (all English and Welsh censuses, with a computer link to the Scottish census of 1881)

- General Register Office for Scotland, Edinburgh (Scottish censuses only)

- National Archives of Ireland, Dublin (Irish censuses only)

Each of these resources is described below. The Family Records Centre is described in detail in the second half of the book.

Local record offices and county libraries

Many local record offices and some county libraries have purchased microfilm copies of the censuses that are relevant to their locality. If you are lucky enough to live near where your ancestors lived, your local record office might be the most convenient place to go to for your search.

A complete list of microform copies of the census held in local record offices and libraries throughout the UK is given in Gibson and Hampson, *Census Returns 1841–1891 on Microform: a Directory to Local Holdings.*

To find out what sources are available in a county or borough library near you, you need to access a service on the internet called *Familia* (http://www.earl.org.uk/familia). This is a directory of family history resources held in public libraries in the UK and Ireland. Each library has provided information on whether they hold any of the following:

- Registrar General's indexes to births, marriages and deaths from 1837 (England and Wales) or from 1855 (Scotland)

- parish registers, 16th to 20th centuries

- *International Genealogical Index*

- census returns 1841–91

- directories 18th to 20th centuries

- electoral registers and poll books 18th to 20th centuries

- unpublished indexes

- newspapers

- periodicals

- photographs

Local record offices and libraries cannot provide the comprehensive resources available at the FRC to help you find your place in the census. Many do hold copies of the surname index to the 1881 census, and will have copies of any finding aids (often surname indexes) created by the local history society. Some of these can be very full. They can be especially helpful if you have drawn a blank in searching for a particular address which your family used but which does not appear in the street indexes. This type of problem can be solved by searching the more detailed records of town planning and building development.

You can find your local record office listed in the local telephone directory. It is best to telephone first before your visit.

Family History Centres

The Church of Jesus Christ of Latter-day Saints (LDS), based in Salt Lake City, Utah, has gathered a huge range of genealogical material both from the official records and through research by its members. You can gain access to this collection at a number of Family History Centres established by the LDS Church throughout the UK. You do not have to be a member of the Church to visit one of these centres, but a small fee is charged. You can find out which is your nearest Family History Centre by contacting the address below. Always contact an individual centre before your visit, to check that it holds copies of the records you wish to consult and to make an appointment.

The main resource available at the centres is the *IGI* and *FamilySearch*, which are described on pp. 48–9. They also hold copies of the surname index to the 1881 census. If you want to consult one of the census returns, a copy is ordered for you from the USA, so this can take a little while. It may still be the most convenient option for you.

▼ The Genealogical Society of Utah
British Isles Family History Service Centre
185 Penns Lane
Sutton Coldfield
West Midlands B76 8JU

Family Records Centre (FRC)

If you live in England or Wales the best resource for researching the census records for the whole of these two countries is the Family Records Centre. The FRC is a service for family historians, set up in 1997 by the Office for National Statistics (ONS) and the Public Record Office. It provides a comprehensive reference resource including indexes to the major sources for family history in the UK, microfilm copies of a wide range of documents including the census, CD-ROM and online search facilities and a large collection of reference books, indexes and maps.

▼ Family Records Centre
1 Myddelton Street
London EC1R 1UW
General telephone: 020 8392 5300
Fax: 020 8392 5307
Internet: http://www.pro.gov.uk/

You can visit the FRC in person without an appointment. If you are disabled, ring first, as there are some disabled parking spaces, but these need to be booked in advance.

Opening times (closed Sundays and Bank Holidays)

Monday	9 a.m. to 5 p.m.
Tuesday	10 a.m. to 7 p.m.
Wednesday	9 a.m. to 5 p.m.
Thursday	9 a.m. to 7 p.m.
Friday	9 a.m. to 5 p.m.
Saturday	9.30 a.m. to 5 p.m.

For more information on using the FRC, see p. 50–60.

The Family Records Centre

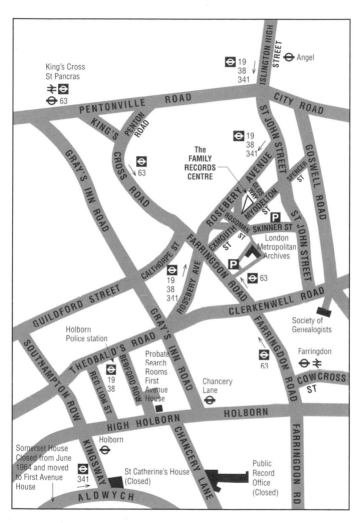

... and how to find it

General Register Office for Scotland

In Scotland the census began under the aegis of the English system but responsibility for it was transferred in 1861 to the Registrar General for Scotland. The records are now held at New Register House. Here you can search microfilm copies of all the original census returns for Scotland and the online version of the 1881 census, together with a range of finding aids and indexes. The online material is accessible for a fee over the internet and at the FRC (see pp. 60–61.)

Only the returns for 1841–91 are available for searching, until the 1901 census is opened to the public in 2002.

The search room at New Register House is open 9.00 a.m. to 4.30 p.m., Monday to Friday. The cost of a full day of searching is currently £17. From 1.00 p.m. a charge of £10 is made for any remaining seats. If you are travelling some distance, it is advisable to book your place, but otherwise booking is not essential since a third of the seats cannot be reserved in advance.

▼ General Register Office for Scotland
   New Register House
   3 West Register Street
   Edinburgh EH1 3YT
   General telephone: 0131 334 0380
   Search room telephone: 0131 314 4450
   Fax: 0131 314 4400
   Internet: http://www.open.gov.uk/gros/groshome.htm

National Archives of Ireland

The establishment of the census in Ireland did not go as smoothly as in the rest of the British Isles. The first attempt to hold a census, in 1813, was a failure. The 1821 census was the first to obtain meaningful results, and thereafter a census was taken every ten years as in the rest of the British Isles, including 1911. The next census in the Republic of Ireland was held in 1926. In Northern Ireland the census continued to be taken at the same time as in the rest of the UK.

Unfortunately nearly all the returns used to compile the Irish censuses have been lost. This was partly through long-standing government policy to destroy them and partly through the destruction of the Irish record office buildings in 1922. Only the records of the 1901 and the 1911 censuses are intact. Some returns still survive for the 1831 and 1841 censuses.

In Ireland detailed information was collected for everyone staying in each household or institution on census night, from the start:

- full forename and surname

- age

- occupation

- relationship to head of household

Information was also collected on how much land and how many storeys belonged to each household.

Those records that have survived are held at the National Archives. They are listed in Gibson and Medlycott, *Local Census Listings, 1522–1930*, together with lists of various other data that have been retrieved or reconstructed.

▼ National Archives of Ireland
Bishop Street
Dublin 8
Ireland
Telephone: 003531 4072300
Internet: http://www.nationalarchives.ie/

PREPARING FOR YOUR SEARCH

The census was not designed to help people trace their family histories and its records were not preserved with future family historians in mind. Do prepare for your search in advance, and don't expect instantaneous success. It can take a while to find your family, but when you do locate their household in the census you will experience a great thrill of excitement. Here is a tangible link with your forebears!

The most important facts you need before you begin are the surname and where your family lived. This is because the census records are organised according to the numbers originally given to the registration districts used for the civil registration of births, marriages and deaths, rather than by the names of the households or people included in the census. You may have picked up this number already, in your search for civil registration records.

District numbers started at 1 in Kensington in central London and fanned out gradually across England and Wales. In this way adjacent places generally, but not always, were given adjacent numbers. Of course this arrangement is not particularly user-friendly to family historians, who would rather search by surname. On the other hand, it is usually fairly easy to find out at least the area where your family was based. Once you have this, the next step is to match it to its registration district number. At the FRC, there are place name indexes to help you do this (see pp. 54–6). In a local collection, the information should also be available.

Research at home

To start with you need to gather as much information as possible from your family. Old documents found in the attic will give you factual information, but even without these you can learn a lot about your forebears from anecdote. What were their names? What was their religion? Were they rich or poor, farmers or artisans? This type of information will give you a context for searching the census.

Old photographs can provide a context for your census
research. Woodcutter's cottage in the New Forest,
20 May 1892 (PRO COPY 1/408)

If you are lucky enough to find documents or memorabilia about your ancestors, scour them for solid facts about the family. A copy of the Bible handed down through the generations can be invaluable, for instance, as many families recorded their addresses and important family events in their Bible. Even old pictures of people you can't identify can yield information – the photographer's address might give a clue to the area where this branch of the family lived.

Check your facts

Once you have gathered all the information you can at home you will be able to draw up an outline family tree, and choose the lines you want to find out more about. The next step is to check the information you have gleaned for accuracy as far as possible. If you rely on the recollections of your relatives alone for dates and places you might be misled into a fruitless search in the wrong place.

The best way to be sure of your facts is to trace them back through the birth, marriage and death certificates derived through civil registration. All give valuable information in pinning down where your family lived. They give information about the registration district where the registration took place, though this may not be the district where your family was on any particular census night. They also give the following additional clues about where the family might have been on census night:

- **Birth certificates** give the place of birth (which was usually at home) and the address of the informant, who was usually the father or mother.

- **Marriage certificates** give the names and addresses of the bride and groom and of their fathers.

- **Death certificates** give the place of death and the address of the informant, who was in many cases the head of the household, and usually a member of it.

ⓘ **Remember**

Your family could well have moved house between registering a birth, marriage or death and the nearest census date. A great deal can happen to a family in ten years. Don't rely on instant success. Take with you all the information you can, in case a more extensive search is necessary!

USING THE CENSUSES: WHAT YOU NEED TO KNOW

Enumerators and registration districts

From 1841, the enumerators (census data collectors) had to distribute the official census forms and collect them when completed. They had to ensure that the heads of households had completed the forms properly, but they did not have to complete the forms or seek the information themselves. They then had to transcribe the information from the forms onto the official enumerators' returns, and check for accuracy when necessary.

Individual enumerators were each responsible for an enumeration district covering only a few hundred households. Enumeration districts were grouped together in sub-districts under the supervision of a registrar, who was, in turn, responsible to a superintendent registrar. The larger areas covered by the superintendent registrars were known as registration districts and were the same as those already established in 1837 for the civil registration of births, marriages and deaths. Although census districts are sometimes called 'parishes', they are in fact quite distinct from Church of England parishes.

Those people staying in an institution such as a prison, a workhouse or a hospital had to be included in a census form completed by its head. Returns also had to be made for those on board ship, whether it was a naval or merchant ship, or just a barge travelling along a canal.

The 1841 census

Although most people had become used to the census, there was great opposition from a variety of sources to the widening of its scope in 1841. Many people were suspicious of the reasons behind the count. They thought, for instance, that

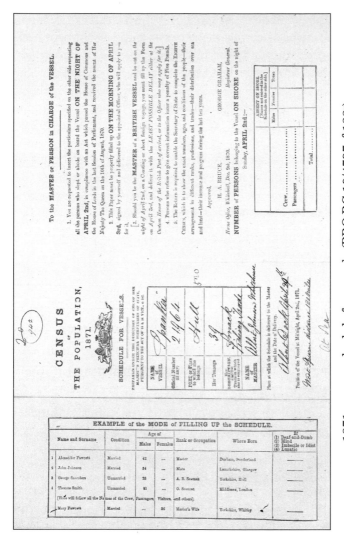

1871 census schedule for vessels (PRO RG 10/4797, f.133ᵛ)

the government must have an ulterior motive, such as tightening up tax collections or reorganising the poor back to their counties of birth. Others objected on religious grounds. It was seen as an invasion of privacy and a threat to liberty. Some people deliberately avoided being included in the census by making a mess of their forms or staying out all night.

The information required in 1841, for everyone staying in each household or institution on census night, was:

- all forenames and surname
- age (rounded down to the nearest five year band for anyone over fifteen years old)
- sex
- occupation
- whether this household or institution was their usual residence
- whether this household or institution was in their county of birth
- if not, whether they were born in Scotland, Ireland or 'foreign parts'
- to which household they belonged, in a building containing more than one household

All this information is obviously invaluable to anyone interested in family history. When you find the household where your family lived, you will open up a wider picture of what they did and how they lived. You will also very likely discover people you did not know existed. But there are a number of problems with this census that you must bear in mind.

Difficulties with data in the 1841 census

- The rounding downwards of adult ages can make it very difficult to use the census as a source of accurate birth information. People also guessed at ages that they were not entirely sure of or deliberately concealed their true age. For instance, a thirty year old woman might have given her age as twenty-nine to the head of household, who would then have rounded it down to twenty-five. Anyone looking for her birth record would automatically be led astray by five years.

- In the section on occupation, the form required only one entry. Many people had significant secondary occupations that went unrecorded.

- The information required about place of birth was only vague.

- People who were out working during the night of the census were mostly left unrecorded.

- As the count was based on households and institutions, it was likely that the homeless were overlooked.

- It is difficult to work out the structure of the relationships in some households where a lot of people had the same surname. Be careful not to make too many assumptions.

The 1851–91 censuses

Many of the inadequacies of the 1841 census were recognised and remedied immediately. By 1851 the following additional information was required:

- the complete address of each household

- exact ages of everyone (not just those under fifteen)

- marital status

- relationship to head of household

- place of birth

- inclusion of any members of the household who were out working at night

- a record of medical disability

At the same time, the date of the census was moved to the spring. This was because summer migrations and late working hours, especially of agricultural workers, had distorted the previous census returns.

In 1891 a few further refinements were made, including allowing space for more information about people's

Administrative County of .... Suffolk

The undermentioned Houses are situate within the Boundaries of the

Civil Parish of Dunwich ... Municipal Borough ... Municipal Ward ... Urban Sanitary District of Dunwich ... Town or Village or Hamlet of Dunwich ... Rural Sanitary District of Blything ... Parliamentary Borough or Division of S.E. ... Ecclesiastical Parish or District of Dunwich

No. of Schedule	ROAD, STREET, &c., and No. or NAME of HOUSE	HOUSES Inhabited	HOUSES Uninhabited	NAME and Surname of each Person	RELATION to Head of Family	CONDITION as to Marriage	AGE Males	AGE Females	PROFESSION or OCCUPATION	Employer	Employed	Neither	WHERE BORN	(1) Deaf-and-Dumb (2) Blind (3) Lunatic, Imbecile or Idiot
1	Mariner House	1		Robert Smithson	Head	M	35		Coast Guard			X	Essex, Laindon	
				Eliza A. do	Wife	M		30					Kent, Dartmouth	
				Edward do	Son		9						Hants, Gosport	
				William do	Son		2					Suffolk, Dunwich	
2	Mariner House	1		Thomas Pitcher	Head	M	30		Coast Guard			X	Essex, Burnford	
				Fanny Pitcher	Wife	M		27					Essex, Bayford	
3	Pitcher House	1		Edward Davis	Head	M	25		Coast Guard			X	Suffolk, Walhall	
				Eliza M. do	Wife	M		22					Cornwall, Falmouth	
				John do	Son		3					do do	
				Thomas J. do	Son		1					Suffolk, Dunwich	
4	Mariner House	1		Bennett Chilton	Visitor	M	30		Coast Guard			X	Suffolk, Colneis Minot	
				George Page	Head	M							Suffolk, Colneis Minot	
				Gordon A. do	Son		4						do, Chatham	
				Gordon E. do	Son		2					do do	
				William do	Son		1					Kent, Walton	
				John J. do	Son		1					do do	
5	Mariner House	1	1&1	William Walker	Head	M	22		Gardener		X		Suffolk, Blythburgh	
				Mariett A. do	Wife	M		20					do, Yoxville	
				Alice M. do	Daug		4					do, Dunwich	
				Alice E. do	Daug		1					do, Dunwich	
6	Cliff House Lodge	1	1&1	John Cooper	Head	M	58		Gardener Domestic			X	Essex, Colford	
				John M. do	Wife	M							Suffolk, Southwold	
				Helen C. do	Daug								London, Mary Newington	
				Sophia M.D. do	Daug								do do	
				Mariett M. J. do	Daug				Domestic Servant			X	Suffolk, Holbeam	
				Elizabeth Bliss	Serv				Domestic Servant			X	Suffolk, Spexhung	
				Phillis	Serv				Domestic Servant			X	Suffolk, Ipswich	
	Total of Houses and of Tenements with less than Five Rooms	6		Total of Males and Females			12	17						

Note.—Draw the pen through such of the words of the headings as are inappropriate.

1891 census return for Dunwich in Suffolk (PRO RG 12/1483)

occupations and introducing (into the Welsh census) a record of what language was spoken in each household.

Adjustments were also made to the size of some census districts in order to ensure a more even distribution of work amongst enumerators. These adjustments have always been kept to a minimum, however, in order to maintain the comparability of the census results over time.

Census dates for England, Scotland and Wales, until 1901

1901	31 March
1891	5 April
1881	3 April
1871	2 April
1861	7 March
1851	3 March
1841	6 June
1831	29 May
1821	28 May
1811	27 May
1801	10 March

A Sunday was always chosen as census day because it was the day of rest and most people would be at home.

SEARCHING THE CENSUS: GENERAL ADVICE

Using surname indexes: the 1881 and other indexes

Where surname indexes exist, these are obviously the easiest way to find people. The 1881 census is so far the only census to have a comprehensive surname index. The index, which is available either on microfiche or CD-ROM, can be seen at most of the usual places where you can see the census (see p. 19).

The 1881 index covers nearly 26 million people. It includes more than just names, to help you match up other known details. It is arranged nationally, and then by county, then by surname and then forename. For each person it gives the following information:

- place of birth
- age
- address at the time of the census
- occupation
- relationship to the head of household
- name of the head of household

In addition the index gives a reference number for each person. Take a careful note of it, as you will need this to find the microfilm of the original census return.

HALLIDAY

, Lucy M

CENSUS DATA © BRITISH CROWN COPYRIGHT 1982.

MICROFICHE EDITION OF THE INDEXES © COPYRIGHT 1990, BY CORPORATION OF THE PRESIDENT OF THE CHURCH OF JESUS CHRIS

SURNAME	FORENAME	AGE	SEX	RELATION-SHIP TO HEAD	MARITAL CONDITION	CENSUS PLACE	OCCUPATION
HALLIDAY	Lucy M.	20	F	Daur	U	Woolwich	Corn Handler
HALLIDAY	Margaret	32	F	Wife	M	Beckenham	---
HALLIDAY	Margaret T.	9	F	Daur	-	Beckenham	Schlr
HALLIDAY	Mary	28	F	Wife	M	Eltham	---
HALLIDAY	Mary A.	58	F	Sis	U	Woolwich	---
HALLIDAY	Mary J.	27	F	Wife	M	Milton In Grav+	---
HALLIDAY	Naomi	23	F	Daur	M	Tonbridge	---
HALLIDAY	Nelly	19	F	Daur	-	Deptford St Pa+	---
HALLIDAY	Reginald M.	3	M	Son	-	Milton In Grav+	---
HALLIDAY	Rose Kate	13	F	Daur	-	Folkestone	Scholar
HALLIDAY	Rosie	8	F	Daur	-	Swalecliffe	Scholar
HALLIDAY	Samuel	38	M	Head	W	Badlesmere	Ag Lab
HALLIDAY	Sarah	40	F	Wife	M	Sittingbourne	---
HALLIDAY	Stephen	73	M	Head	M	Swalecliffe	Publican & F
HALLIDAY	Stephen	30	M	Son	U	Swalecliffe	Carter (AG)
HALLIDAY	Thomas F.H.	7	M	Son	-	Rochester St M+	Scholar
HALLIDAY	Thomas G.	29	M	Head	M	Rochester St M+	Picture Fram
HALLIDAY	W. Herbert	20	M	Bord	U	Margate St Joh+	Assistant Sc
HALLIDAY	William	61	M	Head	M	St Lawrence	Shepherd
HALLIDAY	William	41	M	Head	M	Sittingbourne	Grocer
HALLIDAY	William	33	M	Head	M	Woolwich	Driver Royal
HALLIDAY	William	15	M	Lodg	U	Lee	Gent Serv D
HALLIDAY	William	4	M	Son	U	Greenwich	Scholar
HALLIFAX	Charles S.	3	M	Son	-	Lewisham	---
HALLIFAX	Charles T.	29	M	Head	M	Lewisham	Clerk
HALLIFAX	Eliza	33	F	Wife	M	Plumstead	---
HALLIFAX	F.W.	41	M	Head	M	Plumstead	Labourer In
HALLIFAX	Florence	18	F	Daur	-	Plumstead	---
HALLIFAX	Harry S.	1	M	Son	-	Lewisham	---
HALLIFAX	Henry	13	M	Son	-	Plumstead	Errand Boy
HALLIFAX	John	10	M	Son	-	Plumstead	---
HALLIFAX	Mary A.	29	F	Wife	M	Lewisham	Mistress Emp
HALLIFAX	Wm. Frederick	68	M	---	W	Plumstead	Pensioner Ar
HALLIGAN	Mary	66	F	Inmt	W	Greenwich	Laundress
HALLIGAN	Michael	20	M	---	U	Gillingham	Pte 53rd Reg
HALLIGAN	Peter	41	M	Pris	M	Gillingham	Convict
HALLIGAN	Samuel	45	M	Lodg	U	Woolwich	Potman
HALLIGSON	Thomas	33	M	Head	M	Appledore	Farm Laboure
HALLINGHAM	Henry	45	M	Lodg	U	Allhallows	Agl Labr
HALLION	John	23	M	Son	U	Greenwich	Fireman
HALLION	Margaret Mt.	48	F	Wife	M	Greenwich	---
HALLION	Margaret Mt.	6	F	Daur	U	Greenwich	---
HALLION	Michael	21	M	Son	U	Greenwich	Fireman

Extract from the 1881 census surname index

LATTER-DAY SAINTS.

NAME OF HEAD	WHERE BORN		NOTE	REFERENCES			
				PUBLIC RECORD OFFICE			G.S.U. FILM NUMBER
	CO	PARISH		PIECE RG11/	FOLIO NO	PAGE NO	
ALLIDAY, Eliza	KEN	Woolwich		0744	111	45	1341174
ALLIDAY, John	SCT	---		0849	46	36	1341201
ALLIDAY, John	SCT	---		0849	46	36	1341201
ALLIDAY, Chas.	BEK	Warfield		0728	20	35	1341169
ALLIDAY, George J.	MID	London		0747	13	17	1341175
ALLIDAY, David	IOM	---		0871	124	51	1341206
NION, Thomas	KEN	Tunbridge		0919	46	33	1341219
ALLIDAY, Ellen	ENG	---		0708	66	9	1341165
ALLIDAY, David	ESS	Maldon		0871	124	52	1341206
ALLIDAY, Edward	KEN	Folkestone		1010	28	49	1341240
ALLIDAY, Edward	KEN	Swalecliffe		0965	75	4	1341229
elf	KCN	Hastingleigh		0967	77	10	1341230
ALLIDAY, William	KEN	Chatham		0976	82	10	1341232
elf	KEN	Whitstable	*	0965	76	6	1341229
ALLIDAY, Stephen	KEN	Swalecliffe		0965	76	6	1341229
ALLIDAY, Thomas G.	KEN	Chatham		0887	62	14	1341210
elf	KEN	Chatham		0887	62	14	1341210
DODBOURN, Rachel +	SOM	Yatton		0984	145	28	1341234
elf	KEN	Wickham		0990	123	14	1341235
elf	KEN	Sheerness		0976	82	18	1341232
elf	SUS	Chichester	*	0745	26	1	1341174
AYNE, Charles	NFK	Barnham Broom		0730	72	63	1341170
ALLIDAY, Henry	KEN	Greenwich		0725	8	10	1341169
ALLIFAX, Charles +	MID	Paddington		0738	41	9	1341172
elf	MID	Knightsbridge		0738	41	9	1341172
ALLIFAX, F.W.	KEN	---		0753	98	16	1341177
elf	---	St Lukes		0753	98	16	1341177
ALLIFAX, F.W.	KEN	Plumstead		0753	98	16	1341177
ALLIFAX, Charles +	MID	Paddington		0738	41	9	341172
ALLIFAX, F.W.	KFN	Plumstead		0753	98	16	1341177
ALLIFAX, F.W.	KEN	Plumstead		0753	90	16	1341177
ALLIFAX, Charles +	MID	St Georges Hanover Sq		0738	41	9	1341172
ALLIFAX, F.W.	---	St Lukes		0753	98	16	1341177
-"UNION WORKHOUSE"	KEN	Greenwich		0727	68	19	1341169
-"CHATHAM & ADJ B+	IRE	---		0897	6	7	1341213
-"H M CON PRISON +	IRE	---		0897	75	36	1341213
CANLAN, Grace	IRE	---		0742	52	13	1341173
elf	SUS	Heathfield		0943	21	1	1341225
RADLEY, James	KEN	St Marys		0884	6	5	1341210
ALLTON, Patrick	IRE	Cork		0726	54	4	1341169
ALLION, Patrick	IRE	Clonmile		0726	54	4	1341169
ALLION, Patrick	---	Greenwich		0726	54	4	1341169

There are no overall surname indexes to the other censuses, but there are very many surname indexes covering particular areas. The 1851 census is especially well covered. These indexes are arranged by place (registration district) rather than surname, so you will need to know roughly where your family lived. They have been compiled by family history societies and are an example of just how valuable the work of these societies is. You can check in Gibson and Hampson, *Marriage, Census and Other Indexes for Family Historians* whether there is an index for the place you are interested in. Local holdings of census films are often well indexed.

Searching with a precise address

A precise address is the best information to have when searching for a family in the census, because when you find it you can be certain you have the right people. Many Victorian addresses have changed considerably over the years, as roads have lengthened. Roads, which now have one name and one system of numbering, were previously numbered in smaller stretches as new houses were added. One road (say Lock Road) would be numbered as 1–20 Lock Cottages, Lock Road; 1–4 Myrtle Cottages, Lock Road; Jubilee Lodge, Lock Road; 1–2 New Cottages, Lock Road, and so on. When renumbering took place, with odd numbers on one side and even numbers on the other, old addresses may be misleading. Many small places did not have house numbers at all.

There is a series of street indexes for large towns at the Family Records Centre, which are of enormous help in pinpointing an address in the records. For more information, see pp. 54–5.

If you haven't got a precise address, don't despair – you will find that many indexes and finding aids have been prepared to help you in your search.

Searching without a precise address

Without exact addresses it can be difficult to find your way around the census. This applies especially if your family had a common surname or lived in a large town with numerous census districts. If you know your family lived in a small town or village you might quickly find your relations by looking through the complete return for it. But you might equally find that the village was part of a larger district, which would make searching more difficult.

It is still worth looking in the census even without a precise location for your family. You may find a number of different families with the same surname in the area where you suspect your family was located. Looking through the detailed returns you may find a family that matches what you know about yours. If you don't there are a variety of indexes and finding aids at the FRC to help you. These are described on pp. 53–60.

Interpreting the records

The first difficulty you will almost certainly find when you get the right census return on your microfilm reader screen is literally reading it! You have to get used to reading microfilm and even so the image is not always very clear. This is especially a problem with the 1841 census, which was written in pencil. The other problem is that Victorian handwriting styles were very different to modern writing, and sometimes the enumerators were careless or in a hurry. If a particular word or letter troubles you, carry on reading and go back to it when you have become more accustomed to the style.

Another problem is the use of language to describe occupations. It is very exciting to discover what your forebears did for a living, but many occupations have now died out and the words to describe them have died out with them. You can imagine what a 'clay cutter' might do, but what exactly was a 'journeyman'? What did a coprolite miner actually dig? What was a higgler? Here is an opportunity for further historical research. Finding out about the locality where your family lived, and the work available there, at the time they lived there, can give a real insight into what their lives might have been like. You may well find that a local historian has been there before you, and has published something to answer many of your questions!

Another approach to understanding how occupations were described might be to consult the rules used by the enumerators on how to note them down. These are available in the *Census of England and Wales 1861, Clerks' Instructions for Classifying Occupations and Ages of the People*. The truth is that there was no reliably accurate way of recording occupations so you need to approach this area with a measure of caution.

ⓘ **Remember**

Whatever their trade or station, people would be more inclined to exaggerate their position in society than to understate it.

Do not expect everything you read in the census to be true. Literacy levels were not so high as they are today and spelling was not standard. These factors gave a large margin for error during transcription of the records. Some people were deliberately untruthful and many gaps were left in the information, especially in the early years. Such gaps can be very misleading, so be careful about what assumptions you make.

TRACING YOUR FAMILY BACK THROUGH THE CENSUSES

The exact places of birth given in the census returns from 1851 are invaluable. You can use them to help find the birth records in the civil registration indexes (if they were young enough to have been born after July 1837!). They can even help trace people back to the early 19th century before civil registration began. With the benefit of an exact address, you should be able to locate the parish where your ancestor was born. Then you can look in the appropriate parish register for more records of baptisms, marriages and deaths in your family, or alternatively look again for your family in the *IGI*.

The *International Genealogical Index (IGI)*

The *IGI* is a name index on microfiche arranged alphabetically by county. It contains millions of names gathered from a number of sources all over the world. For the British Isles the primary source of names has been the records of baptisms, marriages and deaths in the parish registers, together with a number of nonconformist registers. Although thousands of names have been included it is important to remember that the index is not comprehensive. It is updated every few years.

The main use of the *IGI* is in searching for people before 1837 when civil registration began, but it can also be useful in locating where your family lived.

FamilySearch

FamilySearch is a computer compilation containing millions of facts relevant to family historians. These facts have been collected from a variety of sources, ranging from the *IGI* to information given by individuals researching their own family histories. The greatest value of *FamilySearch* is for records before 1837. Searching it is easy, quick and addictive!

FamilySearch on CD-ROM can be accessed at LDS Family History Centres, at the FRC, at the PRO in Kew, and at a number of libraries throughout the UK and overseas. It is currently available on the internet in a trial form, at http://www.familysearch.org/

USING THE
FAMILY RECORDS CENTRE

The Census and Wills Reading Room

The census microfilms are located in the Census and Wills Reading Room on the first floor of the FRC. When you enter the Reading Room, you will see an information desk and, nearby, a group of carousels containing instruction sheets. It is worth spending a few minutes here to get your bearings, as the system for looking up the census is quite complicated.

The instruction sheets are step by step guides to set you off on your search. If there is anything you don't understand, the staff at the information desk will be pleased to help. They can offer advice but they can't do the searching for you.

Using census records at the FRC

In order to find the microfilm containing the appropriate census return, you will need to find the appropriate reference number, which will be made up of a series of letters and numbers – these will appear on the microfilm boxes and on the microfilm itself.

What you will need at the FRC

- comfortable shoes for standing and walking around (there is less sitting still than you would imagine)

- as little extra baggage as possible. You can dump coats, etc. in a locker, but you do not want to be weighed down by any extra books or materials as you move around finding indexes and films. When you leave the search room, even just for a coffee, you have to give up your place and take all your belongings with you.

- a note of everything about your family you have found so far

- pencils and paper for making notes of what you find

- your money in a pocket or bumbag rather than a handbag that you will have to carry around

- a map, if possible, of the area you are searching

- concentration – don't bring the children – they'll be bored stiff

Each year's census has a lettercode identifying it, and the table below sets out the lettercodes for each census year:

Year	Code
1841	HO 107
1851	HO 107
1861	RG 9
1871	RG 10
1881	RG 11
1891	RG 12

Within these all-encompassing lettercodes, the individual documents which make up the census returns all have their own unique film reference or 'piece' number. You will need to use the various indexes compiled by the FRC to establish the microfilm reference number for the part of the census you need to view. For example, if you wanted to look at the 1891 census for Hackney the film reference would be RG 12/197. The following paragraphs explain how to use the indexes to construct this reference number for your own particular search.

INDEXES AT THE FRC

The various indexes to the census returns are located in the Census Reference Area. There is a separate bookcase housing the indexes for each census year and to make things even easier the indexes themselves are contained in binders which are colour-coded according to which census year they cover. The colour coding is as follows:

Year	Index Binder Colour
1841	Green
1851	Red
1861	Blue
1871	Brown
1881	Yellow
1891	Black

Surname indexes

If there is a surname index covering the census or area you are interested in, finding people in the census can be very easy. The first thing to do is to check whether there is a surname index for the place you want. Go to the Census Reference Area and find the appropriate coloured binder (e.g. Red for 1851; Brown for 1871) for the census year you are searching. For each census year, (except for 1881) there is a set of binders containing an index to surname indexes – to make locating them easier these binders have blue spine labels. The indexes are not comprehensive and are arranged by place name. Look up the place name where you believe the family to be living at the time the census was taken.

For the 1881 census there is a full surname index for England and Wales – this is described in more detail on p. 41. You can view it either on microfiche or on CD-ROM. The index is national, so even if you're not sure which county you're looking for, you can look through the national index to try to locate your family.

Street indexes

If there is no surname index, check whether there is a street index for the address or place you want. Large towns will have included several registration districts and indeed long streets may have been divided between several different census enumerators. The FRC has spent years creating street name indexes to get round this problem so it is worth checking if one exists for the area you are interested in – they are available for most large towns and cities.

To identify a street index you will need to know the name of the registration district. The registration district can usually be identified from a birth, marriage or death certificate and if you have a copy of one of these documents, it is a good idea to bring it along with you when you search the census records.

Alternatively, the registration district can be found by looking up the place name, e.g. parish, in the place name indexes which have been compiled for each census year. Again, to make locating them on the shelves easier, these are contained in binders with pink spine labels. There is also a separate index to London streets and their localities and these are contained in binders with green spine labels. These can be used to identify registration districts within London.

You can then use the street indexes to look up the name of the registration district on the alphabetical list of street indexes. Once you find the relevant street index number, take a note of it and then consult the relevant street index (binders with white spine labels) and look up the street index number. This will give you an alphabetical list of streets within the film reference you need and the folio (sheet) number to help you find your place on the film.

If you do not have an address,
or there is no street or surname index

First look up the place name you are searching in the place name index (binders with pink spine labels) and note the district number, which is highlighted in yellow, and the sub-district number to its right.

You then need to consult the reference books for the census year you are searching. These are held in binders with yellow spine labels. Use these reference books to look up the district number, highlighted in yellow, and the sub-district number to its right to locate the place-name. The number that appears immediately opposite or above the place name in the far left-hand column is the film reference. You are now armed with all the information you need to collect your film!

Special note about the 1841 Census

The arrangement of the 1841 census was slightly different to that of the others. Each book of census returns had its own number appearing on the title page and on every frame of the microfilm. These numbers make an additional element in the reference numbers to the 1841 census microfilm. The layout of the 1841 reference book is also slightly different from the others with the registration district numbers appearing at the bottom of each page.

If you need to establish a registration district for the 1841 census it is therefore best to look up the place name you want in the 1851 place name index.

---

① **Remember**
Some places were so small that they were included in larger places nearby for the purpose of the census. The main aid for overcoming this problem is the Hamlet Index, which gives the name of the larger place, the county and the registration district. The census did not use the church parish structure that was familiar to people at the time. They would describe their abode in terms of parish: the census is arranged by registration district.

---

① **Remember**
The FRC holds a list of parishes, in which you can find the registration districts of each church parish. There is also a Welsh place name index.

Collecting your film

Once you have established the correct reference number for the microfilm you want, collect a black box from the shelves in the Census Reference Area and note the number on the box – this is your seat number You can then go to the appropriate microfilm cabinet to select your film, putting the black box in place of the film you remove. You are then ready to put your film on the microfilm reader!

Using a microfilm reader

If you feel daunted as you approach the microfilm reader with your first roll of film, don't worry – they are not as difficult to use as they might appear. There are clear instructions near each machine on how to load your film, and there are plenty of more experienced people around to watch. If you do get stuck, a member of staff will help or you could try asking someone who seems to know what they are doing.

As you wind through the film to find your place, you will notice the separate original volumes of the returns, each with a title page describing what is in it. You can check the document reference, which has been added on a strip to every frame.

Some rolls of film are more difficult to read than others. The first step if you have difficulty is to experiment with different adjustments to the magnifier in front of you. You must be prepared to be patient in puzzling out old handwriting. One solution might be to take a copy home to study at your leisure – most people like to take copies anyway. You can also ask staff for help. In extreme cases you may be allowed to see the original, but this requires a special appointment.

ⓘ **Remember**

If you are looking in the 1891 census and don't like microfilm, a microfiche version is available.

Making copies

If you would like to have a copy of the census entries you have found, make a note of the reference number, book number for 1841, the folio number (stamped on every other page) and the printed page number. Rewind your film and then either take it to the Copy Desk or use any of the self-service copiers in the Reading Room.

Can't find your street or family?

If you cannot find a street or your family does not appear in the census at the address you expected, the FRC holds a small collection of maps which may be of some help. The two main collections are Ordnance Survey maps and census registration maps. If you have exhausted all other means of trying to locate the street where you expected to find your family then it may be possible to use some of these sources to identify a particular place. Ask a member of staff for guidance on these sources if you have reached an impasse!

<u>THE SCOTTISH LINK</u>

A Scottish Link is also available at the FRC. Here you can book a computer for up to two hours at a time to search online the main genealogical sources for Scottish ancestors. A fee is charged to use this online service. The Scottish Link is a popular resource so it is advisable to book in advance of your visit. To do this telephone 020 7533 6438.

The census information available via the Scottish Link at the FRC is

1881 census   All the information entered on the original returns

1891 census   An index of the census by name. The
                entries also include age, sex, and the
                registration district and county of the
                household in which the name was
                registered

When you have located the return you are interested in
you can apply for a paper copy taken from the census film.
For the 1891 census you will need to do this to obtain full
information on the household where your ancestors lived.
The information given online on the 1881 census is complete. Contact the General Register Office for Scotland
(address on p. 26).

FURTHER READING

Pocket Guide, *Using Birth, Marriage and Death Records*

C. R. Chapman, *Pre-1841 Censuses and Population Listings* 5th ed. (Dursley, 1998)

J. Gibson and M. Medlycott, *Local Census Listings, 1522–1930, Holdings in the British Isles* 3rd ed. (FFHS, 1997)

J. Gibson and E. Hampson, *Census Returns 1841–1891 in Microform: a Directory to Local Holdings* 6th ed. (FFHS, 1994)

J. Gibson and E. Hampson, *Marriage, Census and Other Indexes for Family Historians* 7th ed. (FFHS, 1998)

J.S.W. Gibson and P. Peskett, *Record Offices and How to Find Them* (FFHS, 1998)

E. Higgs, *A Clearer Sense of the Census* (London, 1996)

S. Lumas, *Making Use of the Census* 3rd ed. (PRO, 1997)

Record Repositories in Great Britain 11th ed. (PRO/ Royal Commission on Historical Manuscripts, 1999)

K. Schurer and T. Arkell (eds), *Surveying the People* (Oxford, 1992)

R. Smith, 'Demography in the 19th Century', *Local Historian*, vol. IX (1970–71)